A Messenger Arrives at a Tudor House

A HISTORY OF HOUSES

R. J. UNSTEAD

ILLUSTRATED BY J. C. B. KNIGHT

A. & C. BLACK LTD

4, 5 & 6 SOHO SQUARE LONDON W.1

BLACK'S JUNIOR REFERENCE BOOKS

General Editor : R. J. Unstead

© 1958 A. & C. BLACK LTD

REPRINTED 1960, 1965 AND 1967

SBN: 7136 0109 4

PUBLISHED BY A. & C. BLACK LTD

4, 5 & 6 SOHO SQUARE LONDON W.1

MADE IN GREAT BRITAIN

PRINTED BY MORRISON AND GIBB LTD., LONDON AND EDINBURGH

An Elizabethan brick-built mansion

CONTENTS

ACKNOWLEDGMENTS

The frontispiece is by Alan Sorrell.

Grateful acknowledgment is made to the following for their permission to reproduce photographs :

　　The National Buildings Record, p. 43.

　　The Marquess of Salisbury and Photo Precision Ltd., p. 47.

Acknowledgment is also made for the use of drawings from John Gloag's *English Furniture* on pages 50, 61, 62, 67, 73.

1. THE STONE AGE

Many thousands of years ago, when Britain was still joined to the continent of Europe, the whole country was covered by dense woods and forests.

The climate must have been much warmer than it is today, for animals such as lions, elephants, and hippopotomi are known to have lived in Britain.

The first men, hardly different from animals, lived along the banks of the rivers.

They fed upon berries, roots, and the flesh of any little animals which they could catch with their bare hands.

They hid in the trees when they saw the larger animals, and their first "home" was probably a shelter among the rocks.

Early man survived because he was cleverer than the huge animals that stalked the earth; plucky and cunning, he learnt to track, to grasp and throw. When he first aimed a stone at a bird or finished off a wounded animal with a stick, he had begun to use tools. Ages passed, however, before he was able to build a home for himself.

Some of these caves, like Kent's Cavern in Devonshire, were very large indeed. We know that they were the homes of cave-dwellers for thousands of years.

Gradually, Britain became colder. A huge mass of ice spread southwards until it reached the centre of England.

CAVE DWELLERS

Animals that love hot weather moved away, and probably most of the human beings also travelled southwards. But some men remained in Britain, living in caves for shelter, and wearing the skins of animals for warmth.

Flint tools, spearheads, darts, harpoons and needles have been dug up from the floors of these caves.

When man learned to make a fire—probably by accident at first—life became a little more comfortable for him. The fire kept wild animals away from his cave, and he could now cook his food.

The story of homes and houses is the story of man's search for greater comfort and safety.

THE FIRST HUTS

The Cavemen were hunters who did not know how to grow crops, or how to keep animals for food. When the wild animals moved away to new feeding grounds, the hunters had to leave their caves and follow them, carrying their weapons and a precious piece of fire in a hollow stick.

Where game was plentiful, the family group made a stop and looked round for a place to light a fire and rest the children out of the rain and icy wind.

If the hunters could not find new caves, they were forced to build shelters.

They pushed branches into the ground in a circle and tied them together at the top.

Smaller branches or reeds were woven in and out, and then smeared with clay, or covered with skins, to keep out the wind and the rain.

The fire had to be made on the ground outside the hut.

7

THE FIRST ENCAMPMENTS

About seven or eight thousand years ago men first began to keep tame animals, and to grow crops.

They no longer hunted for all their food. This meant that people could live in more settled homes, and in larger groups or families.

But they still had to move from time to time to seek fresh pastures for their flocks and herds.

At night, the animals had to be protected from enemies and wolves, so a fence of stakes was built round the camp. The huts were used only for shelter and as sleeping places. The fire was still outside.

These camps were made on the grassy hills of the Downs and uplands. The river valleys were marshy or thickly-forested, and wild animals lived in them.

Stone Age men avoided the low-lying land and made their way along the hills.

2. THE NEW STONE AGE

PIT DWELLINGS

In the New Stone Age, men learned how to grow crops by scratching the chalky soil with flint hoes and antler-picks. They built homes of stone, which lasted longer than shelters made from branches and skins.

They built a low circular wall of stones, leaving a gap for the door. A strong post was driven into the centre of the floor to support the branches of the roof. The roof was covered with grassy turf.

Inside the hut, they dug out the earth to a depth of two or three feet, and piled it outside. Thus the floor of the house was lower than the ground outside, rather like some old cottages which have a step down from the street. This made the hut less draughty, and gave more head-room inside.

The circles of earth and stone remained on the hills long after people ceased living in pit-dwellings. " Hut-circles " can still be found in many parts of Britain, usually on high ground such as the moors of Devonshire and Yorkshire.

The fire could now be made on a flat stone inside these big huts, and the smoke found its way out through the door, or between the roof branches.

Inside the hut a number of large stones made a low platform or couch. This probably served as a bed when it was covered with skins.

9

WATTLE AND DAUB HUTS

If there were no stones to make a wall, the New Stone Age men set up a ring of posts. They tied poles from them to the big post in the middle.

The walls were made of a kind of basketwork called wattle, smeared all over with wet clay. This method of protecting a house from wind and rain is called " wattle and daub."

Home was a single-roomed hut in which all the family slept and sheltered. Work and cooking were done out of doors.

For hundreds of years men made houses like this even when they had learned much better ways of building.

Around a cluster of huts men dug a ditch and built a fence to protect themselves from their enemies.

Thus they began to live in large families or tribes, under the leadership of their Chief.

3. THE BRONZE AND IRON AGES

LAKE VILLAGES

The tribes of the Bronze and Iron Ages were constantly at war with each other. Some men began to build their homes on lakes or marshes, so that they should be safer from their enemies.

A famous Lake Village was built at Glastonbury in Somerset. Here, an island was made by driving hundreds of poles and tree-trunks into the mud, and by piling up earth and stones until the " floor " was solid enough to build on.

The wattle and daub huts were thatched with reeds, and each had a flat hearth-stone. The stone sometimes sank into the soft floor ; then another was placed on top.

All round the island was a strong fence, to prevent the banks from crumbling into the water. At night the gates in this fence were shut and barred.

There was a landing-stage for boats, so that the villagers could go to their fields and flocks on the mainland.

Tools of stone, iron and bronze have been found at Glastonbury, as well as bracelets, rings, pots, and millstones for grinding corn. Weaving combs and spindle-whorls show that these people were able to make cloth.

A Lake Village

4. HOUSES IN ROMAN BRITAIN

In the West and the North, and outside the towns, most Britons continued to live in the same kind of homes as their forefathers had done.

But they were able to enjoy many of the goods which were brought by traders who followed the Roman legions.

The Ancient Britons lived in wattle-and-daub thatched huts, which were usually grouped together in settlements, protected by a strong fence, earth banks and ditches.

When the Romans settled in Britain, they built homes similar to those in Italy, and in many parts of their Empire. At first, these new houses were built for the Roman officials and business men.

In the South-East, British chiefs and wealthy merchants soon began building similar houses for themselves, so that they could live in the Roman manner.

The Romans thought that a civilised person was one who lived in a town. They knew that town-dwellers could be made to pay taxes and obey the law, since life in a settled community led to trade and peaceful living.

Therefore, when Britain was conquered, towns were built in many places, usually near a former British settlement, and at some important point, such as a cross-roads or a ford.

The Romans built their roads, towns and houses to a careful plan, which was always neat and regular.

A Street in Roman Britain

A TOWN HOUSE

The entrance to a town house was often a plain doorway between two shops. The visitor, shown in by the porter, or door-keeper, was greeted in the Courtyard or Atrium, a pleasant wide room with a marble basin or pool in the middle.

On each side were small rooms, some for house-slaves, and others for visitors and members of the family. There was also a chapel, and perhaps a library.

Right Plan of a Roman Town House

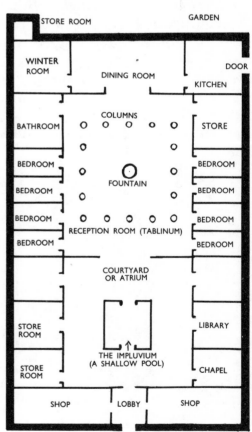

A Covered Walk or Corridor

Sometimes there was a specially heated room for use in the winter, since Roman officials found Britain very cold.

The Roman houses had a most ingenious method of central heating. On the concrete base of the house were built short pillars or piers, each with a large square tile as a cap. Across these small tiles were placed larger tiles, to make a solid floor.

In a big house there might be a second court beyond the Atrium, open to the sky, with a fountain in the centre of a little garden. Round the courtyard were low walls with short columns supporting a tiled roof, making a covered walk or corridor. The biggest room leading off this corridor was the Dining-Room (Triclinium). There were also bedrooms, a kitchen, bathrooms, and lavatories.

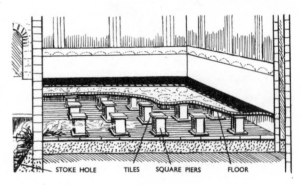

STOKE HOLE   TILES   SQUARE PIERS   FLOOR

A Hypocaust

Then a fire, usually of charcoal (which gives very little smoke), was lit in the stoke-hole outside and warm air passed under the floor and up the sides of the room, through hollow tiles.

This heating chamber (called a hypocaust) can be seen at Verulamium (St. Albans), where a Roman floor has been cut open to show the piers and the hollow tiles.

A Courtyard or Atrium

The floors themselves were usually very handsome. They were made of hundreds of tiny coloured stones set in cement and arranged to make patterns or pictures. They were often beautiful works of art.

The coloured stones—black, red, orange, grey, and white—were cut into small cubes, the smallest for the craftsmen employed in the richest homes.

The walls of the houses were usually covered with fine plaster, and gaily painted with patterns or pictures of gods and goddesses.

Some artists painted clever imitations of marble, which would be used to give an exceptionally rich appearance to the house.

A Mosaic Floor

The finest room was probably the Triclinium or Dining-Room. Here Romans of the highest class took their meals reclining on low couches, round a central table.

But probably only a small number of aristocrats, and those who copied them, ever dined in this uncomfortable way.

Slaves cooked the food in the kitchen, on a raised hearth in which there were several shallow holes for charcoal fires. Over the holes pots and pans were placed, as they are on a modern gas or electric stove.

Ovens were seldom built, because Romans preferred their food boiled or fried.

THE ROMAN COUNTRY HOUSE OR VILLA

As the country became peaceful and settled, a number of large villas were built, especially in southern Britain. They were probably built for rich officials, and officers of high rank who had retired from the army.

The Roman villa was really a gentleman's country house. It was surrounded by his farm or estate, which produced much of the food needed by the many people who lived at the villa.

(On the opposite page is a picture of a Roman villa.)

The villa often had an outer fence, or wall, as a protection against runaway slaves and robbers. Passing through the gatehouse in the wall the visitor found himself in an enlarged version of the town-house.

Ahead of him was the open courtyard, with its statue or fountain in the centre. The visitor would see, on at least two sides, a covered walk with pillars. The slaves' quarters would be on the left hand side (as in the picture) ; the Dining-Room, main rooms, stores, barn and kitchens would be opposite the main gate.

To the right of the main gate were the bathrooms. There were warm and hot rooms, and last of all was the Frigidarium, with its cold bath, big enough to plunge into.

A Roman Villa in Britain

The villa itself was built of brick or of two-foot thick concrete walls, but the upper storey seems to have had a timber frame filled in with wicker and daub.

So the outer walls, unless they were covered with plaster, looked rather like those of a Tudor house. The roof was usually tiled, but slates or even thatch may have been used at times.

Thus, for a period of three hundred years, there were houses in Britain as fine as any that have ever been built. They had central heating, glass windows, and luxurious baths, and the rooms were large and had beautiful floors.

After the Romans left, hundreds of years passed before men built houses that could be compared with the villas of southern Britain.

5. SAXON HOMES

After the Romans left, Britain was gradually overrun by the heathen warriors who had for many years been attacking the East coast.

The new settlers—Angles, Saxons and Jutes from across the North Sea—were vigorous fighters and sturdy farmers, but they had no understanding of town life, or of gentle living. It is quite likely that they feared the spirits of departed men who had inhabited the Roman dwellings ; at all events, they made no attempt to use these dwellings.

The towns and villas fell into decay, and were broken up for use as building materials. Later, the ruins became hiding places for robbers and outlaws.

WOODEN-FRAMED HUTS

The Angles and Saxons made clearings in the forest for their fields, and for their new homes. The homes were still like the earliest kinds of shelter.

Boys camping in a wood have often made this kind of frame for a shelter.

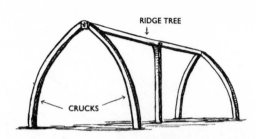

The Angles and Saxons chose two curved trees and split them down the middle to make the end timbers. Then they joined them by a ridge pole, which sometimes needed a centre-post for extra strength.

The early houses had a frame like that of a barn. Upright posts gave the house straight sides, and the spaces between these posts were easily filled in with wattle and daub to make the walls of the house.

This was called " post and pan " work ; if part of the wattle was left out, the space between two posts made a " window-pan," which is why we still speak of a window-pane.

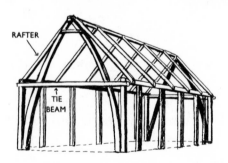

The post in the middle of the house was a nuisance, especially if a fire was wanted, so a beam was put across the house, and the centre-post could then be cut down. A short post called the " king-post " rested on the cross beam, and helped to support the roof.

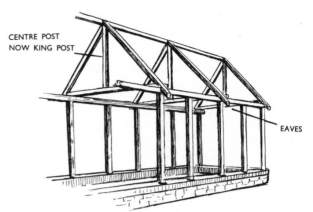

Later, the frame of the house looked like this.

This simple kind of construction, with wattle and daub " pans " and thatched roof, was used by the Saxons for their houses and barns.

THE CHIEF'S HUT

The Chief, of course, had the largest house in the settlement or village.

As you can see, the timber frame was clearly visible, and the windows were no more than narrow slits. The gable ends were often decorated with dragon heads, similar to the prows of the long ships, since these Norse warriors tended to think of a house as an upturned ship.

19

Inside the Chief's house or hall, there was little decoration, save for a few antlers on the wall. Even the weapons that hung there were ready to be snatched down if an alarm was given.

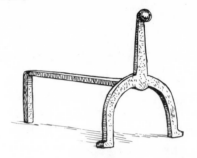

A Fire-dog

Here lived the Chief and his warriors, eating and resting when the day's work was over, or feasting and singing after a successful raid on a neighbouring Chief.

The huge stone hearth was in the centre of the hut. On it burned a fire of logs supported on an iron

fire-dog. In the ashes at the side, food might be kept warm, but cooking for the Chief was done in a small hut outside.

The smoke found its way through the eaves and out of a hole in the roof. This hole was often protected by its own little roof, as in the picture at the bottom of page 19.

The Chief, his wife, and close companions, sat at the top of the Hall, and the warrior-farmers were seated at trestle-tables down each side of the long, dim room. This left the middle clear for the fire, for the serving men (often slaves captured in battle), and for a minstrel or harpist who entertained with songs of glory.

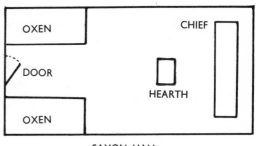

SAXON HALL

The Saxons used oxen for ploughing, and looked on them as most precious possessions, so the oxen (four in a team) were often stabled in a bay at the end of the Hall.

Doors, made from strong planks, were usually open by day to allow light to enter the Hall. Early hinges might be made from a wooden or iron pin that allowed the door to turn in holes on the door frame, (as you will still find in some Italian cupboards today).

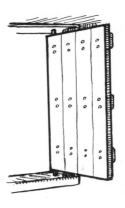

A Pin-Hinge

But a better hinge was an iron bar with a ring at one end which fitted over an iron hook on the door post. This sort of hinge is still in use today.

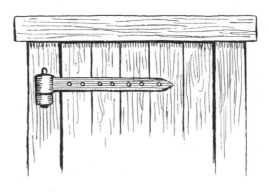

The Chief's Bower

It is clear that there was little comfort in these smoky, draughty Saxon halls. There was no light at night, except from the flickering fire and from wooden torches dipped in resin (a tree-gum that burns brightly).

Men wrapped themselves in their cloaks and fell asleep in the bracken or reeds that littered the floor.

The Chief would withdraw with his family to the "bower," which was either a separate hut, or a room at the end of the Hall.

The Chief's bed was built of rough planks against the wall, and was more like a large box or cupboard.

The children would be lucky to have a straw pallet on the floor.

While the Danes were settling in Eastern England, and during King Alfred's great reign, houses changed very little. (We know how draughty Alfred's royal residence must have been because his candle clocks had to be protected by lantern covers with windows of thin horn).

However, stone was being used for building some churches, monasteries, and fortifications, as well as for the houses of powerful thanes.

When Alfred re-built London, he used some of the stones of the ruined Roman town.

A PEASANT'S HUT

The farmers, husbandmen, and poor peasants continued to make their homes in the old way; a simple wooden frame was filled in with wattle and daub.

They made the daub by mixing chopped straw and clay into a stiff paste.

(Notice the room for the animals at one end of the hut.)

6.   HOUSES IN NORMAN TIMES

The Battle of Hastings gave William I a kingdom, and he took good care that he did not lose it.

Fortified wooden towers were raised to dominate the countryside, and very soon afterwards stone castles were built wherever a strong point was needed.   William's barons held these castles.

King William divided the land of England between his barons, and the barons paid homage to him for it.   In the same way, the barons gave lands to their Knights, and received homage from the Knights.

CASTLES AND MANORS

The castles and manor houses built by the Norman lords consisted of one great Hall, and they were not very different from the Saxon dwellings.   Stone and flint were used more frequently, but many of the smaller manor houses were still built of timber with wattle and daub between the posts.

In this picture of the Great Hall in an early Norman castle, you can see the lord seated at one end, with his table on a platform or *dais*. His followers are seated at trestle-tables on either side of the central fireplace.

A Norman Fireplace

The smoke found its way out of the small, round-headed windows, and out of a smoke-hole in the roof, protected by its cover. (The cover was called a *louver*.)

Presently the fireplace was made against an outer wall. Then the smoke escaped, not up a chimney, but through flues cut in the thickness of the wall, coming out on each side of a buttress.

A Fireplace, Showing the Flue behind it

As you can see, there was little comfort or decoration. The windows had no glass, and only wooden shutters to keep out wind and rain.

Sometimes a frame was made with a lattice of criss-cross strips, the forerunner of diamond-paned windows.

25

THE MANOR HOUSE

An Early Norman Hall

The Normans built manor houses with the hall on the first floor, for greater safety. The entrance was by an outside staircase. The ground floor, called an undercroft, was a store-room.

Since a fire could not be placed in the middle of a timber floor upstairs, a fireplace was made against the wall with a chimney to carry off the smoke.

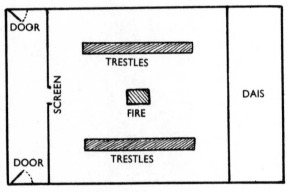

Plan of the Hall

By the twelfth century the hall was usually on the ground floor again, and stood in a walled courtyard, apart from the kitchen and out-buildings. There was a dais at one end for the lord's table, and, at the other end, a screen to reduce draughts.

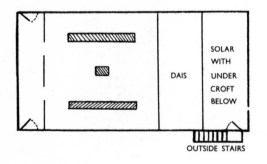

Servants and retainers took their meals in the hall and slept there at night. For the lord's comfort, a private room, called the *solar*, was added behind and above the dais.

Since the hall was lofty, the solar was built as an upper room, reached by a staircase outside. There was a store-room beneath the solar, as you can see in the plan at the bottom of page 26.

The stairs to the solar were sometimes covered in as a protection against bad weather, and later the solar could be reached by a ladder from the hall. Henry III ordered a staircase to be built to replace the ladder in one of his houses.

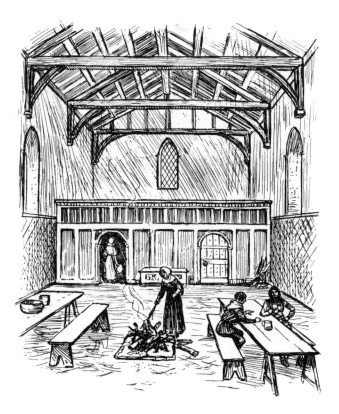

The far end of the Hall looked like this when seen from the dais.

Notice that the screen now has *two* doorways. Above the screen a gallery for musicians would one day be built.

The Solar

There was a fireplace and a bed with side curtains. There were no cupboards, but poles standing out from the wall to hang clothes on.

Next to the solar there was frequently a chapel for worship by the lord and his household.

A washing room and a lavatory were sometimes added, and, occasionally, even a bath.

The most important articles of furniture were the bed and the chest.

THE SOLAR

The solar was the bedroom and sitting-room for the lord and his family. Already, it was far more comfortable than the Hall. Its window, if upstairs, was bigger to let in the sunlight.

THE KITCHEN

Food was cooked in a building outside, and carried into the great Hall. This must have been very inconvenient, so an early improvement was to add two rooms at the " screens " end.

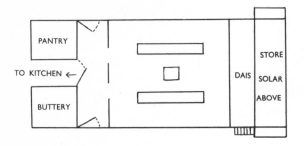

These were the *pantry* (food store) and *buttery* (drink store for wines and ale). A passage between them led in to the kitchen.

This passage to the kitchen was eventually covered over to prevent the food getting cold. Later still, the kitchen was added to the house.

One reason why the kitchen remained a separate building for so long was that the large number of people livir g at the Manor required a big room in which to prepare and cook their food.

In the picture below is a fortified Manor house with its kitchen still separate, though the pantry has been added. You can see the steps leading to the solar.

THE VILLEIN'S HUT

The villeins continued to live in wattle and daub huts, or cotts, which they built themselves with help from neighbours. The fire was still made on a hearthstone in the centre of the room, and the only light came in through the door.

The pigs had a sty next to the cott, but the " best beast " usually had a stall inside the hut.

The villeins built their cotts close together, near the church and stream. Each villein had his little vegetable garden, but his strips of farmland were scattered, and some distance away.

A Norman Village

7. THE LATER MIDDLE AGES

In the later part of the Middle Ages houses were slowly improved.

Windows became bigger ; you remember that the Normans built rounded arches with the window cut in the thickness of the wall. During the Middle Ages, building styles changed, and arches became pointed. Windows were larger, with strips of masonry dividing them into two.

Glass was very costly. Even in the houses of rich men it was set in a frame that fitted into the window space, so that the frame could be taken away if necessary. The lower part of the windows opened like a door (this is called a casement window).

To hide the rough stone, the walls might be plastered indoors. Plaster was made by mixing powdered limestone, or burnt chalk, with water, and then strengthening it with straw or animal hair.

In monasteries, where the monks constantly kept the bare patch (or tonsure) of their heads shaved, and their hair cut short, they saved their own hair for mixing with the plaster. The smooth plaster was painted with bright colours.

A Norman Window

In wealthy homes the walls were hung with tapestries, skilfully woven to depict hunting scenes, old legends or Biblical scenes.

Tapestry was often called " arras," because the town of Arras in France was particularly famous for weaving tapestry.

THE BARON'S HALL

In this picture of a medieval baron's Hall, you can see many of the improvements which have taken place in the three or four hundred years after the Conquest.

People grew tired of going outside to the staircase to reach the solar so they made a trap-door with a ladder indoors, and this led to the making of a staircase in the corner of the hall.

The central hearth has disappeared, and the fireplace is against the wall, though you cannot see it here.

Notice the handsome screen, and the new staircase leading to the Musicians' Gallery above. The walls are hung with tapestries, and an outer door has its own screen.

The tables are laid with cloths, and the guests are not rough warriors but ladies and gentlemen—at least, in appearance! The only improvement in furniture, however, is a high-backed settle at the top table, and it is probably the only seat with a back on the entire manor.

The jester is a member of the household, kept by the lord to amuse guests with his antics and songs.

The boy waiting on the far side of the table is a page. He is a nobleman's son who lives with this family to learn the manners and correct behaviour of a great household. When he is older he will be a squire and will follow his lord into battle.

The manor house was now far more than one great Hall, though the Hall was still the centre of the house, and of all that happened.

The household continued to take their meals here, and justice was given at the Manor Court.

Many rooms had been added to the hall, such as the chapel, kitchen, and solar.

Bedrooms and a winter parlour became part of the house, and sometimes the rooms were added above the Hall itself.

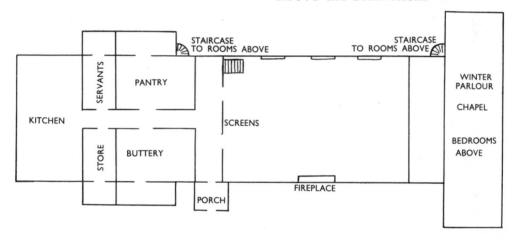

THE KITCHEN

There might be as many as fifty persons living in a manor house, so the kitchen was a very busy place. Enormous quantities of meat were eaten, and two or three fireplaces were needed for roasting and boiling it.

Often the meat would be slowly turned on a spit over a log fire.

A scullion or kitchen boy would be set to turn the handle, and baste the meat from time to time.

Ovens came into use at this time. They were very big, and were used for baking bread, pies, and cakes.

In the winter salted meat would be stewed in big cauldrons slung over the fire from a hook in the chimney.

The Winter Parlour in a Noble's House

TOWN HOUSES

In the Middle Ages more and more people began to live in towns. The towns were small and were surrounded by strong walls.

Since it was not safe to live outside the protection of the walls, houses were built as close together as possible, and the streets were no wider than alley-ways.

Only the main road from the town gates was wide enough for carts and wagons. In these crowded towns, houses were usually built with their gable-ends facing the street.

Often, houses were joined together, sharing a " party " wall. By law, this wall had to be three feet thick, and made of stone, because of the danger of fire. But the rest of the house had a timber frame.

Rooms had low ceilings, so that a tall man could hardly stand upright. Often the ground floor was dug out a foot or two below street-level to make the house less draughty and the rooms higher.

Houses leaned towards those opposite, and it became common to build *upwards*, adding a room above the first floor, because there was no space to expand a house sideways.

A Merchant's House

Soon people could lean out of a top floor window and shake hands with a friend across the street !

Why were houses built like this ? The ground floor was built on a timber frame, then cross-beams were laid for the next floor.

If you wanted to make quite sure that this second floor was firm, you would lay your beams so that they came right across the lower frame. In fact, the cross-beams projected a little beyond the upright posts.

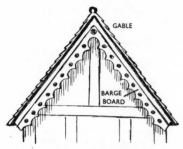

The spaces between the timber frame were filled with wattle and daub, and then covered with plaster.

Sometimes, to give the house a handsome appearance, patterns were made on the plaster while it was still wet : this work is called " pargetting."

The gables of town houses were also decorated by placing a carved board, called a " barge-board," as an edging to the roof. The projecting beam-ends were often carved with faces of men and animals. Carved water spouts, called gargoyles, gushed water from the mouth of a hideous creature.

Most shopkeepers and business men worked at home. They did not put a notice outside their shops, for few people could read.

Instead, they hung the sign of their trade—a boot, a barber's pole, or a large glove.

Traders tended to dwell together, so it was easy to tell what goods might be had in Glovers Row or Baker Street, Goldsmith's Street and Mercery Lane (a mercer was a cloth merchant).

A Gargoyle

The merchant or craftsman worked with his apprentice in the ground floor room, and people came in through his open door to see his goods.

He might also put a stall outside, or let down his window shutters to serve as a counter.

Here you can see how narrow and dirty the medieval streets were, and how people built their houses as they pleased. They added a storey when necessary, or tacked on an attic room that projected crazily over the street.

In the fourteenth or fifteenth century the parlour of a well-to-do trader, a prosperous goldsmith perhaps, would look like the one shown above.

Because the tradesman used the ground floor as his workshop, he had his parlour upstairs. Here he took his meals, and entertained his friends and visitors.

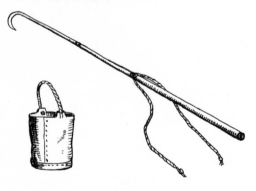

A Bucket and Fire Hook

The room, reached by a steep stair from the shop below, was lined with thin sheets of wood called panelling or *wainscot*.

There was a handsome stone fireplace with an iron fireback, and a chimney made of stone, or even of the new bricks which had recently come from the Low Countries. The settle had a cushioned seat as well as a back.

The danger of fire was so great that the Mayor ordered the merchant always to have ready on the wall outside a leather bucket full of water, and a fire-hook to pull off smouldering thatch.

There was probably only one other room on this floor, the master's bedroom.

Here stood his most cherished possession, his bed, with its feather mattress, bolster and handsome curtains.

Here was the baby's cradle, and perhaps a truckle bed on a low frame for an older child, or for the maidservant.

In this room too, was kept the family chest, containing money and important papers such as title deeds to property and marriage settlements, for there were no banks yet where valuables could be stored in safety.

If more bedrooms were needed for servants and other children, then the roof had to be pulled off, and another storey added to the house.

(The apprentice lads, of course, slept as best they could in the shop downstairs.)

A Fifteenth-century Mansion, timber-framed on a brick foundation

The fireplace was no longer in the middle of the floor, but was at one side. It had an iron or stone fireback to prevent the wall catching alight.

Cooking was done in the warm ashes, and in the pot which hung from a chain attached to an iron crane set in the wall or fireback.

A woven hood led the smoke out of the smokehole, and the hood was smeared with clay and cow-dung to make it fairly safe from sparks.

A loft under the roof was used to store winter food and spare implements.

POOR PEOPLE'S HOMES

The peasant's draughty cottage had few improvements, and it was still built exactly as his forefathers had built for hundreds of years.

It was a miserable home, but gradually the peasant began to improve it.

He still stabled his valuable ox, or his only cow. But he made a wattle partition to divide the living-room from the bower, or bedroom. In the bower the family slept on pallets of straw or bracken.

8. TUDOR HOUSES

Fashions in houses do not change rapidly, but there are certain periods in history when a great many new houses are built. (One of these periods followed the 1939–45 war.)

There was peace in the country during most of the reigns of the Tudor monarchs. The merchants, shopkeepers and farmers were more prosperous, and they built new houses.

The quarrelsome barons were exhausted after the Wars of the Roses, having lost their money, power, retainers, and families. They could not consider building houses. But in their place came the upstart nobility who had been rewarded by Henry VIII with the lands of the monasteries.

Tudor Town Houses

We must not forget that, although houses in Tudor times had many similar features, every man was his own architect. He built just as he pleased, and used the ideas and local materials which suited him best.

In many cases he built so well that his house is still being lived in today, as we can see at Lavenham and Kersey in Suffolk, for instance, and in many other places, especially in Gloucestershire and the West Country.

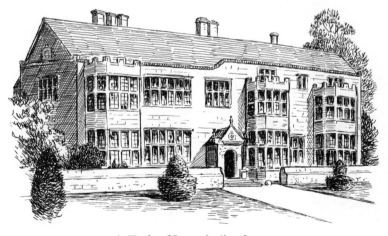

A Tudor House built of stone

41

MATERIALS

There was still plenty of timber for house building though there was some alarm at the rate at which the oak forests were disappearing.

The great trees were carted to the timber-yard and placed over the saw-pit, where the " top sawyer " and the " bottom sawyer " cut them into planks.

Next, the rough planks and posts were smoothed by a tool called an adze.

Very often a natural tree-trunk was built into a house, provided it was the correct size for a beam or upright post.

Using an Adze

Oak was the favourite timber for building because of its strength. Iron nails do not last well in oak, so timbers were jointed and secured by wooden pegs. The exposed beams of Tudor houses were not black but grey.

When the timber was ready, the framework of the house was built up in the same way as in the late Middle Ages.

Each floor jutted out a little from the storey below. Most houses were two storeys high, though a mansion might have a third floor.

In this picture of the framework of a Tudor house, you can see that the chimneys and the base of the house are made of brick.

Stone was used when it could be obtained locally, as in the Cotswolds, Devon, Yorkshire and Scotland.

Bricks originally came to England from Holland in the fifteenth century. They were brought here by the boats which came to fetch English wool, and they were very useful in East Anglia where there was a shortage of good building stone.

Tudor chimneys were particularly handsome. Most roofs were still thatched, but slate and clay tiles were beginning to take the place of thatch, except on cottages.

As timber became less plentiful, and as men wanted to build chimneys for their houses, bricks began to be manufactured in England in the fifteenth century. Many large houses and colleges were built of brick: Cardinal Wolsey's great palace, Hampton Court, is one of the finest examples of brick buildings.

Tudor Chimneys at Hampton Court

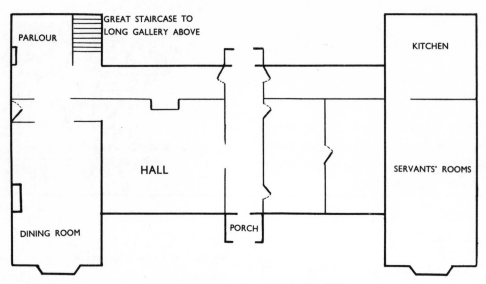

PARLOUR

GREAT STAIRCASE TO
LONG GALLERY ABOVE

KITCHEN

HALL

SERVANTS' ROOMS

DINING ROOM

PORCH

THE GREAT MANSION

When the country became more peaceful, strong castles and houses built like fortresses were no longer needed. In any case, gunpowder could blow up the strongest walls.

Many people now built themselves large mansions standing in private parks. Some men had been given, or had bought, land that once belonged to the monasteries. Some had enclosed the common land and the field-strips for their sheep, and so had made themselves rich.

Other men had grown wealthy from trade or business or royal favour. These were the new lords of the manor who built fine mansions of timber, brick and stone.

The Great Hall of Saxon and Norman days had not yet disappeared, and a hall was built in the new mansions, even though they now had many other rooms.

At the top of the page is a plan of the ground floor of a great house, and on page 3 is a picture of an Elizabethan mansion.

You will see that the great mansion has now become longer. Rooms have been added to the Hall, which is therefore less important.

Also the whole building is regular, and balanced in plan ; each wing that juts out matches another wing on the other side. This is called a symmetrical plan.

Notice, too, the porch in the middle, which helps to give the impression of a capital E lying on its side. This was a fashionable plan in Elizabeth's reign, though it is doubtful if it was meant as a compliment to her.

Great landowners and nobles often built their houses round a central courtyard, which was entered through an impressive gateway.

But although most of these Tudor houses had a regular plan, they were built in a pleasant style, which is peculiarly English and which has never entirely lost its popularity. Notice, in the picture above, the great window to the right of the door which breaks the regularity of the front.

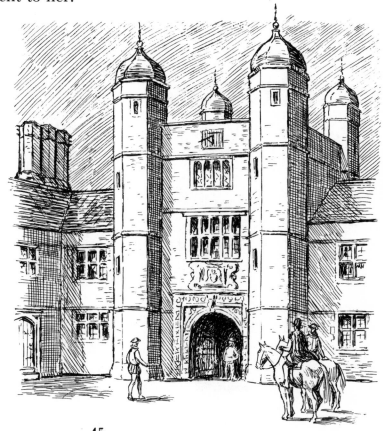

A Tudor Gateway

WINDOWS

Elizabethan windows were most beautiful. Times were safer and glass was plentiful, so for the first time in our history men felt that they could let in daylight, and they allowed their fancies to run riot.

It was still impossible to make large sheets of glass, so the diamond or square panes were set in lead strips, supported by stone uprights (mullions) and cross-bars (transoms).

The Hall, Hatfield House

Inside the great house there were many interesting additions to comfort.

THE HALL

In the picture you see the " show-place " of the great house, used on important occasions, and to entertain royalty to banquets. The long tables and benches remained unchanged from earlier days, but the floor was made of black and white tiles, or paved with slabs of stone.

The walls were covered both by panelling and by fine tapestries. There were also framed portraits— a sure sign of wealth.

At the end of the room can be seen two doors leading through the screen. Above is a gallery for musicians. At the other end, the screens go up to the ceiling, but behind the screen is a passage from which the ladies could look through peep-holes to see whether the gentlemen were staying too long over their wine !

47

The fireplace was made of stone, handsomely decorated, with an ornamented iron fireback (called a *reredos*). The logs burned in an iron basket. Ceilings were decorated with ingenious patterns in plaster.

Beyond the Hall, were the Parlour, and the Dining-Room.

The Hall was two storeys high, but there was ample space upstairs for bedrooms, library, chapel, and the long gallery. To reach them, splendid wide staircases were built.

The craftsmen of the day were highly skilled in handling wood, and these staircases, richly carved with all manner of figures and fruit, were beautifully made.

The main upright posts are called *newels*, and in this picture there is a cupid or a strange animal on each newel.

Notice the little gates to keep the hunting dogs from running upstairs.

The Long Gallery

The fine staircase led into the Long Gallery, which was one of the chief glories of the house. The Gallery ran the whole length of the house, and served many purposes.

Here the ladies walked for exercise on wet days when mud would soil their long, costly dresses. (Remember that ladies were energetic creatures who rode, hunted and shot.)

Here, too, the children played, and took their lessons in Latin and Greek from their tutor, who may have been the family priest or chaplain.

At the fireplace, or striding up and down, the gentlemen in ruffs, doublets and hose discussed politics, voyages, and the latest news from Court.

The Tudors loved music; in the Long Gallery the whole family would gather to sing or to listen to the music of the lute, the viol, virginals or recorder.

The young ladies and gentlemen too, took dancing lessons from their master. The dances were complicated and needed much practice.

D

This book is mainly concerned with the building and layout of houses, but it is impossible to overlook the furniture of the time.

Only the beds were made for comfort, and few chairs had padded seats, or backs, even in the noblest home.

Most of the furniture was made of oak, and it was very strong. But oak cannot easily be carved into graceful shapes, so the furniture was solid and heavy.

The chest had been an important piece of furniture since Saxon times. The Tudors improved its simple design by carving decorative doors, and making it into a cabinet, or by adding drawers, so that later it became a " chest of drawers." Some beautiful sideboards were made in Tudor times.

A Formal Garden

GARDENS

In the Middle Ages, only Kings, nobles, and monks knew the delights of a garden. Chaucer mentions flowers, and we know that roses, lilies, sunflowers, violets and ornamental trees were grown, but a garden was not generally thought necessary for a fine house.

In Tudor times there was a new interest in gardens. Houses tended to be regular (or symmetrical) in design, and men still thought that walls should guard a house. Therefore the gardens, like the houses, were extremely neat, with clear designs and clipped hedges all round.

The garden itself was set in a frame, with the main paths straight, and with little paths curving inwards to make a regular pattern. The flowerbeds were quaintly-shaped, and all were bordered by tiny " hedges " of box, lavender, thyme, or marjoram.

Larger hedges, usually of yew, were clipped into all kinds of odd shapes ; this is called *topiary* work. These neat, patterned gardens are known as formal gardens.

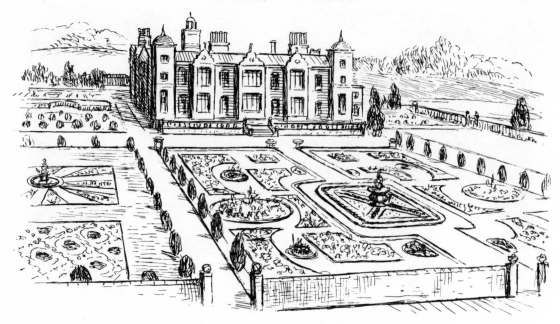

Travellers brought new plants into
the kingdom ; sweet-smelling herbs
were very popular, and grapes,
oranges, and apricots were grown
in sheltered places.

The Tudors had a boisterous sense
of fun. They planted mazes to
amuse their guests, and arranged
hidden fountains which squirted
water over passers-by !

The Tudors probably liked to look
at their symmetrical gardens from
the upstairs windows of the Long
Gallery ; then they could see and
enjoy the pattern of the paths and
flower-beds.

ORDINARY HOMES

So far, we have considered the houses built by the rich landowners, and, generally speaking, it is these which have lasted to the present day.

But, although many men were poor, there was also a class of well-to-do yeoman-farmers and shopkeepers. Some of their snug family houses can still be seen in Stratford-on-Avon, Plymouth, and other towns and villages.

Like the wealthy folk, ordinary people improved their houses. They took out the wooden shutters and the piece of oiled linen which had let in so little light, and added bigger windows made of diamond-shaped panes of glass.

Fireplaces with brick chimneys made it safer to add an upper room over the parlour.

Soon, the rough ladder was replaced by a short steep staircase, with a rope fixed to the wall for use as a banister.

When a farmer decided to add a brick fireplace to his farmhouse, he usually built it at one end of the parlour, like a little room.

The fireplace, with seats on either side and the fire in the middle, was called an Ingle Nook. Perhaps you have stood in one of these great fireplaces and looked up the wide chimney to see the sky?

A Brick Fireplace seen from the Outside

53

Poor people, such as peasants and labourers, did what they could to improve their cottages. In the picture above, the gamekeeper has put a plastered hood over his stone fireplace.

At the end of the room he has made a loft over the outside stable, with a way in from the living-room. The loft is the children's sleeping-place, as well as a store for apples and vegetables!

The floor was not yet paved, but was made of beaten earth hardened with bull's blood. In winter, bracken on the floor made it warmer.

As we have already said, brick chimneys made it safe to build rooms upstairs, even in quite humble houses.

The slope of the roof, and the rafters, were both clearly visible.

There were no corridors upstairs, so each room led into the next.

Furniture and household possessions were still scanty, though ordinary folk now had a larger stock of pewter plate, pottery, and table-linen. Carpets were still expensive luxuries.

In well-to-do-houses, the ladder was replaced by a staircase, and the stairs came from the kitchen or parlour.

The stairs were often made to turn spiral-fashion round a strong central post, because a spiral staircase took less room and was cheaper to build than a straight one.

An Elizabethan country house

9. THE SEVENTEENTH CENTURY

Entrance to a Jacobean Mansion

JACOBEAN AND STUART HOUSES

Styles of building did not suddenly change when James I came to the throne.

But travel abroad began to give men new ideas about buildings. Houses became plainer, and stone and brick were often used instead of timber.

JACOBEAN AND STUART HOUSES

A Jacobean House built of brick and stone, showing the quiet regularity of its front

Many of the favourite features of Tudor houses, such as turrets, mullioned windows, and the grand staircase leading to the Long Gallery, were used for many years.

Until Stuart times, a man built his house as it pleased him. If he were rich, he employed his own master mason and carpenter to advise him. But now the architect appears on the scene.

INIGO JONES

Inigo Jones was the first important architect in our history ; he designed some buildings for James I and Charles I, and his ideas influenced many other builders and architects.

Inigo Jones travelled in Italy, where he liked the buildings which copied the style of the Roman or classical temples. (These buildings are some-times called Palladian—after a man whose name was Palladio.)

A Seventeenth-century Staircase

The pediments are rounded and pointed alternately.

Notice the columns (called pilasters) against the face of the building, and the plain front.

Instead of the great Tudor gateway, the door is elegant, and in harmony with the regularly spaced windows.

The Banqueting Hall, Whitehall

Inigo Jones built the handsome Banqueting Hall in Whitehall for James I. From this very building James' son Charles I stepped on to the scaffold.

The only decorations are the balcony and sculptured fruit at the top, and the "gables" (called *pediments*) over the windows.

A GENTLEMAN'S HOUSE IN THE TIME OF QUEEN ANNE

By the end of the Stuart era, smaller houses were built in a most lovely and elegant style. Here is a Queen Anne house—you may often see similar houses in the older parts of country towns.

The beauty of this house depends upon what is called "proportion." It is both balanced and simple.

In these houses, there was a small hall inside the front door. A glass panel was placed above the door to provide light when the door was closed. Since the bars holding the glass were spread like a fan, this was known as a *fan-light*.

Do you remember that the earlier glass windows opened like doors, and were called "casement" windows? In the seventeenth century, windows that opened by pushing half upwards or downwards became fashionable. These are called "sash" windows. Now that it was possible for glass to be made in larger sheets, the leaded diamond-panes were rarely used.

A Fan-Light

A Casement Window

A Sash Window

Linen-fold Panelling

The stairs, known as "dog-leg" stairs, led straight up from the hall to a landing, and then turned upwards again.

Walls were covered with thin wooden panels called wainscoting. The Stuarts, as well as the Tudors, liked carved panels.

There was a particularly handsome type of panel called "linen-fold," in which the wood was carved to look like pieces of folded linen. You may see linen-fold panelling at Hampton Court and at Hatfield House.

Probably it was meant to contrast with the glorious wood-carving of such men as Grinling Gibbons. (Sir Christopher Wren employed Gibbons to decorate not only the choir of St. Paul's Cathedral, but many other churches and houses.)

In later Stuart houses, the panels became larger and quite plain.

Rich carving, often in the form of rich clusters of fruit and flowers, was placed above doors and fireplaces.

"Sea-coal" was now being used instead of wood, so fireplaces became smaller. The fire itself was contained in an iron basket or grate.

STUART FURNITURE

In Tudor times a gentleman's house had only a few stools, chests, a table, and one high-backed chair. But a hundred years later, the furniture was much more varied and far more comfortable.

Now there were sets of chairs, up-holstered with cushions or padding; sometimes they were seated with cane, or they had rushes woven into the centre.

As well as the large dining-table, small tables were required for card-playing, and for the new habit of tea-drinking.

Mr Pepys loved buying books and so, like the gentry, he needed book-cases in his house.

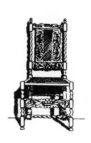

The chest of drawers had two or three drawers. Sometimes a glass-fronted cabinet was added to the top of the chest of drawers, to show off the family's silver plate, and pieces of china from France and the East.

Four-poster beds, with their carved headboards and beautiful hangings, were more elegant than ever, and they were still the most valuable possession in the house. One lady is supposed to have paid £10,000 for her bed !

Formerly, only kings, queens, and nobles had their portraits painted, but now it became common for any well-to-do merchant to hang portraits of himself and his wife on the walls. Mirrors, called " looking-glasses " were also hung.

HOUSES IN THE COUNTRY

In the country, the poorest peasants lived in miserable hovels. But prosperous farmers, yeomen and craftsmen such as the blacksmith, lived in trim cottages, sometimes with " cob " walls two or three feet thick.

These better houses were timber-framed or made of stone ; in the eastern counties they were built of brick. The kitchen, with its wide fireplace, was the principal room of the house.

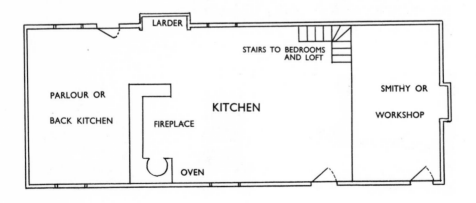

Since a brick chimney could safely be built in the centre of the house, there might be a parlour on one side of the kitchen, and a smithy or a workshop on the other.

There was more comfort in the parlour, with a high-backed chair for the master of the house, and perhaps a dresser to display the pewter plates.

CHIMNEY TAX AND WINDOW TAX

Just when houses were becoming lighter and more airy, the Government taxed chimneys and windows. This meant that the poor people had to do without chimneys, and the smoke from their fires drifted out as best it could through the smoke hole in the roof.

A house-owner with more than six windows also had to pay tax. This did not affect the poor, who certainly had fewer than six windows, and who could not afford glass anyway. They used paper soaked in oil, to let a little light into their two-roomed cottages.

If a man could not pay the tax on his windows he had to brick them in. You can still see houses today where the windows were bricked in during the seventeenth century.

Homes were also workshops. The weaver and his family all worked together in their cottages; tailors, saddlers, smiths, glovers, and shoe-makers made their goods, not in a factory, but at home.

10. GEORGIAN HOUSES

THE GREAT HOUSES

Now we come to the most glorious age of house-building in our history.

Great wealth, gained from our increasing trade, led to the building of vast country-houses. They were splendidly laid out, with parks and gardens, and each employed a small army of cooks, servants, grooms and gardeners.

Blenheim Palace, completed in 1722 by Vanbrugh

The great houses were stately buildings, in the " classical " style, with pillared fronts. They also had many stables, since this was the age of the coach and carriage. The houses were plain yet imposing outside, but they were magnificent inside.

A splendid entrance hall was necessary to receive guests. There were also salons, drawing-rooms, card-rooms, state bedrooms, dining-rooms, and library, not to mention kitchens, servants' quarters, attics and bedrooms, pantries, cellars, linen and china rooms !

ROBERT ADAM

The great architect of the eighteenth century was Robert Adam, who not only designed houses, but also planned every detail of the interiors. He even designed the fireplaces and the furniture.

The Entrance Hall in a Georgian Town House

A room in the Adam style

Adam used curved walls and alcoves, and pillars covered in fine plaster which was painted in delicate colours with gilt decoration.

The ceilings were particularly beautiful, and Italian artists were brought into the country to paint ceilings both with patterns and with pictures. From these ceilings hung wonderful chandeliers made of hundreds of pieces of glass ; they reflected the light from dozens of fine wax candles.

William Kent was another notable architect. His great creation was Holkham Hall, for the Cokes of Norfolk.

Chinese vases and tea-cups (without handles) were popular, and they led to a fashionable interest in Chinese-style furniture, hangings, and expensive wallpapers.

Fine pottery was made in Chelsea and Staffordshire by Josiah Wedgwood and other great potters. They often used designs taken from classical vases.

The fireplace of white marble now had its coal fire in a decorated grate. Notice the Roman or "Etruscan" vases on the mantelshelf.

A " Ha-ha "

GARDENS

Fine houses needed a fine setting. But as if to contrast with the formal style of the great house, the " natural " country or parkland was brought right up to the house.

An extraordinary character known as " Capability " Brown (he invariably remarked that he saw " capability of improvement " in an estate) was the leading expert in this art of laying out grounds. From his gardens the house was seen down an avenue of trees and, often, across an ornamental lake set with fountains.

Little Greek temples might be seen on artificially erected mounds, and statues peeped from among carefully planted clumps of trees.

Thousands of pounds were lavished upon the laying-out of estates for the gentry.

Parks were stocked with deer and prize cattle and, since nothing so vulgar as a fence was allowed to interrupt the view, a hidden ditch, called a " ha-ha," was dug in front of the house to prevent the animals from roaming on to the lawns.

The interest in Chinese articles could be seen in the garden, too. Some people built little summer-houses in the Chinese style, like the one in the picture below.

Adam Furniture

FURNITURE

Georgian furniture had to be in keeping with the expensively decorated Georgian rooms. Oak was sturdy enough, but it could not easily be made into elegant furniture.

This led to the use of walnut, and then of mahogany, a foreign wood from the West Indies. These woods not only took a high polish, but they allowed a new art, called veneering, to develop.

A veneer is a thin sheet of beautifully grained wood, glued on the surface of furniture made from less expensive woods. Patterns and pictures were made by gluing veneers together like a jig-saw puzzle.

In the eighteenth century, three men became famous for their skill in making furniture. Their chairs, tables and sideboards were more delicately shaped and graceful than any ever seen in England before.

These men were Chippendale, Heppelwhite and Sheraton, and examples of their art may still be seen in museums, antique shops, and in some homes.

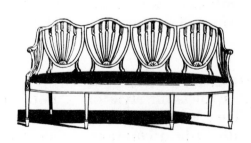

Chippendale

Heppelwhite

Sheraton

FAMILY HOUSES

What changes were to be found in the houses of ordinary, well-to-do people of the towns and country?

Generally speaking, the houses were built in the quiet, pleasant style of Queen Anne. They were of pink or yellow brick, with little decoration, and they looked solid and comfortable.

The houses were large, for many families had several servants, as well as ten or more children. Iron railings were now fashionable in the town.

But, also in the towns, an ever-increasing number of poor people lived in dreadful hovels and slums, without water, sanitation, or any of the decencies of life.

In the country, houses were built of brick and stone. It was also common to cover the timber frame of a cottage or farm-house with overlapping planks, called *weatherboards*. In East Anglia, particularly, these white-painted houses are often seen near mills and malt-houses built in the same style. By the sea, fishermen tarred the boards of their cottages to keep them water-tight like their boats.

Weather Boards

Sometimes tiles were used to keep the rain out, not only on the roof, but also on the walls. Then the house was said to be tile-hung.

A Tile-Hung House

Of course, the poor still lived in their little cottages. They helped out their low wages on the farm not only by spinning and weaving, but also by wood-turning, basket, lace, and clog-making, and a dozen other things, according to their skill and the district they lived in.

Basket Making

Even the smallest children were expected to help earn a few pennies by these cottage industries.

69

11. THE NINETEENTH CENTURY

REGENCY HOUSES

A Regency House

From about the middle of the eighteenth century, a change took place which continues to this day.

People began to grow tired of one style of house-building ; some of them had plenty of money but not much taste, and they wanted something new, something different from their neighbours.

So gradually the steady develop-ment in the plan and appearance of a house was lost. (But only very gradually, for building fashions change much more slowly than ladies' fashions.)

JOHN NASH

At first, there was little change. Regency houses are lovely build-ings, and John Nash is the best-remembered architect of the time.

A Crescent Built in the Early Nineteenth Century

Nash liked to cover his buildings in plaster or white stucco, which led to the rhyme :

> " But is not our Nash, too, a very
>   great master ;
>   He finds us all brick and he
>   leaves us all plaster."

But Nash had a good sense of plan and order, and the London squares were dignified and regular. Houses, windows and shop fronts were curved.

A liking for curves led to the building of town houses in crescents (" crescent " means shaped like a new moon). There are famous crescents at Bath and Brighton.

A Regency Shop

A " Gothick " Mansion

" GOTHICK HOUSES "

A man called Horace Walpole made a tour of Europe in the eighteenth century, and came home full of enthusiasm for Gothic architecture. This was the style in which men built cathedrals during the later Middle Ages.

Walpole built himself a " Gothick " house with pinnacles, turrets and pointed arches, and many other people built similar houses.

VICTORIAN HOUSES

The " battle " between Gothic and classical styles went on through the nineteenth century, but by Victoria's reign, Gothic had almost won the victory.

It is rarely possible to imitate the past successfully ; that is why so many Victorian houses are unbelievably ugly. At the top of the page is a picture of a big house built in an imitation of the Gothic style.

The medium-sized family villa, built in similar style, is even more absurd.

Every kind of unnecessary pinnacle, spire, and turret was added to the outside of the house.

A Victorian Home

Like the outside of the house, the inside was usually fussy. It was crowded with pieces of furniture, and the shelves and the cupboards were decorated with all sorts of knick-knacks.

Nothing was plain, and everywhere there were twirls, knobs and bobbles, as you can see in these pictures.

This kitchen range (the tap at the side is from a water tank heated by the fire) was downstairs in the basement below street-level. Here the servants and cooks worked in ill-lit rooms from which they carried dishes and trays upstairs to the dining-room, as well as cans of hot water to every bedroom.

Many people were poor, so servants were plentiful and were paid very low wages. No thought was given to their comfort.

Bathrooms were only to be found in the homes of wealthy folk : most well-to-do people used a wash-stand in their bedroom, and bathed in a " hip-bath," which afterwards had to be emptied into jugs and carried downstairs by a servant.

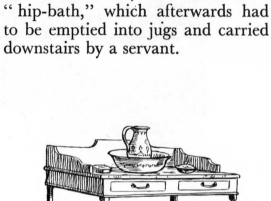

A Wash-Stand

A Hip-Bath

VICTORIAN SLUMS

During the nineteenth century the number of people in Britain increased at an enormous rate. The poorer parts of towns, especially of London and the grimy factory towns of the North, were dreadfully overcrowded.

The slums were whole districts of courts and narrow alleys flanked by houses that were dark and filthy. They had no sanitation, and the only water came from a single tap shared by several families.

Every room, no matter how cold or damp, was crowded with people. Sometimes four families, one to each corner, lived, ate, and slept in a single room.

A Slum Court

No wonder disease, illness, and crime were widespread.

Many townfolk tried to improve conditions by building workers' houses. These were an improvement on the slums, but row upon row of mean little houses, with two rooms upstairs and two down, made our factory towns drab and ugly.

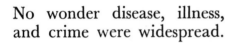

Thousands of these houses are still lived in today, but many of them have been improved, with taps indoors, electric light, and, sometimes, with bathrooms.

A Poor Street in a Factory Town

In Victoria's reign, these little "villas" were given "Gothic" decorations. You must have seen many houses like the one on the left.

Houses were usually lit by gas, and water was laid on only to the kitchen sink. On Monday the copper was heated for the family laundry, unless the house was grand enough to have a brick wash-house in the "yard."

THE SUBURBS

As the centres of towns became overcrowded, new districts called "suburbs" were added to the outskirts. In the suburbs many houses were built in rows, for people who were reasonably well-off.

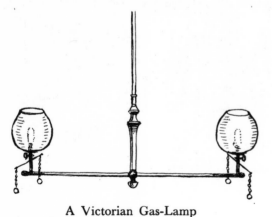

A Victorian Gas-Lamp

This pushing-out of towns from the centre has gone on steadily in the twentieth century. The first suburbs became shabby and old-fashioned, so many people moved out farther still. New suburbs were built in what had formerly been open country and farmland.

12. THE TWENTIETH CENTURY

The great mansion and the huge country-houses have had their day. The large buildings of our times are blocks of flats, offices, or factories.

A Block of Flats

A Modern House

Modern factories and schools are made largely of concrete and glass (rather like Hardwick Hall, built in 1590, in Elizabeth I's reign; in those far-off days, it was called " Hardwick Hall, more glass than wall ").

Tired of the over-decorated, fussy Victorian house, people often wanted no decoration at all. They build houses like cubes, although flat roofs are not very suitable for our climate.

A School in Hertfordshire

77

Ribbon Development

The great advance in twentieth-century housing has been in improving the interiors of ordinary houses by installing electric light, hot water, bathrooms, and reasonable heating.

But in design and appearance our houses have hardly improved at all. From the outside, they are very nearly as drab as their fore-runners in Victorian days : look at these houses on a new estate.

Today, one great problem in Britain is how to house people pleasantly in an overcrowded island without losing all our countryside for many miles around the towns.

Garden cities and " new towns " such as Stevenage, Crawley, East Kilbride, and Harlow, help to solve the problem.

One of the difficulties is that Englishmen (and, undoubtedly Welshmen and Scots too) like gardens, and dislike living in blocks of flats. This is one reason why " ribbon development " (houses built along main roads) has been so popular, and why so many housing estates are built with dozens of identical small houses, each with its tiny garden at back and front.

We have not developed a gracious style of our own in the twentieth century. For this reason many architects, especially in the new towns, use a variety of old and new styles in an attempt to break the monotony of vast housing estates.

Semi-detached suburban houses, built in the nineteen-thirties

Windows in modern houses tend to be larger, often reaching almost to the floor, and glass bricks are used inside and out to make houses seem larger.

Many houses are made to seem light and spacious by having as few dividing walls as possible on the ground floor. The " dining space," for instance, may be separated from the sitting-room merely by a sliding partition, or light shelving for pottery or plants.

In America, houses have been built almost entirely of glass. They have only one room, with a central fireplace and bathroom. In the huge round room are spaces for eating, sitting, and sleeping. Does this suggest that we shall return to a twentieth-century tribal hut, with central heating and with modern comforts ?

Building styles on a modern housing estate

INDEX